POETING THERAPOETICS

by

Deluke Muwanigwa

COPYRIGHT @ 2021 POETING THERAPOETICS
by Deluke Muwanigwa

.

Published by Poetry Planet Book Publishing House
Arranged by Tess Ritumalta
ISBN;
Softbound/Paperback-978-621-8261-77-8
Hardbound-978-621-8261-78-5
Mobile/Kindle-978-621-8261-79-2

Photos used were taken from Pinterest and may contain their own copyrights

DEDICATION

I would like to dedicate this collection of poems to all humans. Fellow humans. May you find peace in sitting down and writing your thoughts until you are understood. There is therapy in writing and the more you write the more others understand your viewpoint. This leads to more understanding and more peace.

ACKNOWLEDGEMENT

I would like to acknowledge those who think I am a bit weird writing poem after poem but are kind enough to let me be. To let me mess around with the Queen's language conjuring up new words, images, and metaphors. When a writer is writing they are said to be writing. When a poet is writing a poem it is fair to say a poet is "poeting". Part of the title of this book is derived from this unfairness in the Queen. I mean the Queen's language.

Poetry is a form of healing. Why else would mentally challenged exponents like me keep poeting when no one seems to care (no one except the millions of other crazy poets poeting away their lives). When I feel strongly about something I write a poem and immediately feel relief. That is a relief. That is therapy. Therapeutics of poetry. Therapoetics of poeting. Poeting Therapoetics. I hope you enjoy this book of therapy. I did writing it.

I would like to thank all the people who put up with me and my poetry. I am glad, though, that now and then, my poem seems to find resonance with their soul and I get a favourable word of encouragement. My Barbie Doll...my wife is one of them. She is the first person whose phone I pester with my drafts. As you can imagine there is war in paradise if she says she is too busy. My daughter also gets disturbed by her busy schedule. I send her few appropriate ones. Being a good daughter, she gives me good high marks.

My gratitude goes to Poetry Planet Publishing House for the actual work of publishing. I am all talk. Poeting...and they are the action heroes and heroines, publishing. Madam Tess Ritumalta. Most importantly I want to thank you the reader of this book, for, a poem becomes a poem when it finds a reader. Otherwise, what's the point. Happy poeting and may you find therapoetics in poeting.

PREFACE

I believe poetry is a form of healing. Just writing your thoughts on paper can go a long way in settling an unsettled mind. There is therapeutics in poetry. Therapoetics.

I believe in fairness. If a writer is writing, then a poet is poeting. Fair is fair.

This book is a collection of poems I found therapy in writing. I have tried to steer away from things political...with difficulty considering our world...and focused more on wordplay. I hope you enjoy reading this book of poetry.

TABLE OF CONTENTS

POETING!

The shock of my life
In my mind the strife
A hoodlum throwing stones
Is not eating scones
A teacher scribbling a pen
Is not insane
The hoodlum is rioting
The teacher is writing

A poet writing a poem
Well, is writing poetry
The poet not poeting
The pen is pointing
To the paper, therefore writing
Poets let's be fighting
To have one word to describe
One verb in trade to ascribe

Tell them you are poeting
When you write poetry poeting
The Thesaurus to say poeting
When you write that rhyme poeting
You recite that prose poeting
Sing that song you are poeting
From today fellow poets poeting
Poeting! Poeting! Poeting!

Forward with the poeting struggle
Poeting to the dictionary we smuggle

THERAPOETICS OF POETRY

Is it just me or you also feel what I feel?

How writing a poem can set you free?

Maybe your thoughts are making you feel morbid

Maybe you are afraid of catching Covid

When you get a blank piece of paper

Write your thoughts your fear tapers

When someone behaves; treats you badly

Take a pen and paper and write madly

When you are done raving and ranting

Even nature upon your peace she's granting

So, when you feel the pent-up anger

Your blood pressure high, you in danger

Don't you dare pick up that loaded gun

Don't you sulk denying yourself some fun

Some problems are best left to the maker of human
beings

The supreme being, the maker of all things

For relief trust the therapeutics of poetry

Have belief in the therapoetics of
poetry.

BLUE MOODS

Some days the blue cover of the sky comes crushing down
I try to soar in time to catch my breath in the violet range.
My wings are melted halfway to the sun with ultraviolet rays,
I fall flat on my back hapless.

On a clear teary day, I swallow the blue oceans to quench my disappointments.
Whatever stroke I try I cannot swim out of my mire, every stroke sinking me in a quagmire
Everything I touch turns to salty water immiscibly blending my tears.

As if that's not enough grayscale living, on some other days I just feel blue. Failing to come to terms with the blueness of my movie-like existence. Thank God I can hide in the rhapsody of the prosody of poesy, a state in which the universe in verses is always green in beautiful colours of the rainbow. Poetry lifts my blue mood sky high.

A LITTLE ALLITERATION IN ACTION

I won't live believing leaves can be used for healing
feelings.

I know not if no knowledge exists in Bollywood,
Hollywood, or Nollywood,

Bastions of make-believe where comic relief allows the
dead to relive leaving us believing, but, deceiving,

That life is like a knife at night it finds spite to spike your
dreams despite sleeping tight and right and inspite of
sleeping in white light.

Seeing is believing but it's hard to hark the bark of the
dog and mark the lark in the yard in the dark.

The lark will take flight at night you might have sight on
site right there and think you're right.

But I caution precaution
A little alliteration in action
Is not useful in this world.
It's just a play on words.

Like, "She sells seashells!" Why get old in the cold as
told, why not fold your hold be bold and, behold,
instead of shells, sell cod.

Unless you say, today it's just a play on words to stay
gay another day, pray that day is not Mayday the first of
May like today.

THE TIME OF MY LIFE

I can't be everything to everyone
I win some, I lose some
Politicians want my loyalty
To eat and live like royalty

Friends want my commitment
To follow the ten commandments
My spouse wants devotion
No talk of divorcing

The government
Their covenants

My employer
The worst spoiler
Like I was born to serve him
There's no time for me

And yet life is short
In comparison, a flitting moment at this earthly port.
Let me be
I wanna be free

Give me time
Time to shine
Give me space
Away from the rat race

I don't have light-years in this form
Only a few years to reform
When I tell you I am writing a verse
Don't be averse

That is my time
The time of my life.

MINE

They came sometime
On a chartered flight
They came at night
Their schedule tight
And stayed out of sight
But, wanted to show their might
That they were bright
They spoke about stalagmite
We knew it was stalactite
We tried to draw a line
At that very time
We tried to be kind
Keeping in mind
That we were in a bind
We needed lime
We needed iron
We needed a good life
We needed our isle
To develop into an island
We were gripped by ire
When the person we hired
We could not fire
Turned out to be a liar
Wanted the entire pyre
The furnace in its entirety
That, we did not like
We did not take to it kindly

So, we refused to sign
A solicitor we had to find
But we lacked finance
The straw was final
When the foreigner finally
Refused to pay a fine
Said he wanted to remind
That we were being unkind
The agreement we could not rewind
We cried
We tried
He lied
That we were tied
But this didn't fly
We asked why
He would try
To have an eye
On our pie
We said by the by
We will bid him bye
This he did not buy
He sighed.
And said wryly
"No need to fight"
"Read the sign"
"Actually, the mine is mine"
"It's all mine".

A PLACE TO HIDE

Are you oppressed?
Are you depressed?
Unfairly treated?
Unduly restricted?
Do not brood all day
Here is how I play

In my time of sorrow, poems provide comfort
The cheerfulness of my stanza comes forth
When I have a strong point to get across

A poem carries the burden of my cross
When I feel the coldness of the human soul
I clothe my verses with the warmth of a song

In agony, I send an "SOS" with rhymes
Carrying a message of healing to all tribes
No matter what danger the world imposes
I rescue myself with verse upon verse of prose
In poetry, I have found a place to hide
In poetry, I can hitch a personal ride

A POEM

A poem keeps the psychiatrist at bay
Therapoetics of poetry at play
Saying things pleasing
Saying things teasing
Laughter the best medicine you won't say

A poem

Paul wrote a poem and sent it to a forum
The poem earned Paul a rap on the forearm
When Paul saw what had been done
He laughed his lungs out wrote another for fun.

A poem

A point of view in a poem is unique
P-oems help you avoid the clinic
O-ne having a literal soliloquy
E-nding the doctor's so-long queue
M-ake a poem your therapy for life

A POET

I would rather be the ocean than a river.
A river though a prolific life-giver
will eventually sink in my bosom
As an ocean, I hold secrets more awesome
Within me resides the wonders of creation
Some to be discovered some extinct under regression

I would rather be the universe than the earth
In the universe resides the Creator and secrets of my
birth
I would carry secrets of planetary formation
particles and energy and their aboriginal information
The earth is an infinitesimal speck of dust
So small it can melt in me completely with crust

I would rather travel at the speed of light
than watch the sluggishness of life
measured in infinitesimal units of years
Instead of multiples of light-years too complex for ears
At warp speed, I would travel to all corners of the
universe
Understanding the music of the spheres in form and
verse

If all these wishes fail me
I would rather just be a poet

A POET

A poet

A man crossed oceans to be a poet
He ended up being just a cohort
His poems sucked
Lousy poems are still to pour yet

And poetry

Clever tried his hand at poetry
He thought it is just to pour a tree
With a bucket of water, he came to PH
Never read a poem even by Lawrence, DH

A poet and poetry

A person who writes needs pity
Penning thoughts in a ditty
Only those who can't converse
End up their speech they convert
To a few verses called poems
And pretend it works for 'em
Now picture this fact
Due to lack of tact
People turn to pen harassing
Only to say things embarrassing
Ending in shame

To most people, it's the same
Reading and writing poetry
You just need a poet and poetry

A POET NEVER DIES

Of course, he dies
Let's not tell lies
But used as a metaphor
It is true therefore

In the beginning of the world
There was a word
The word gave life
And the word poetry alike.

At the end of the earth
We will face death
The poet's work
Will live beyond the word.

Metaphorically
Categorically
A poet never die
Though a poet will die

A POET'S HEART

A poet's heart is at its peak
When a poet can freely speak
Quietly in verse and prose
For a certain noble cause
Never to shout and shriek
Verses loaded with emotion thick

A poet's heart is at its peak
When a poet an idea they tweak
To make a different point
A sheep instead of baaa! goes oink!
Horses growing wings
Just to spruce up things.

A poet's heart is at its peak
When freely moving in the street
Observing the world going round
Writing what's really on the ground
Free of unwanted censorship
And meddling dictatorships.

A poet's heart is at its peak
When at the end of the week
They have written good poems
Someone reads and calls 'em
To say write some more and more
A poem moved them to the core

A poet's heart is at its peak
When a poem someone it reached
Made a difference in their life
Showed many are in similar strife
When a person gives a testimony speech
A poet's heart is at its peak.

A POET'S PLANE

I am living on a poet's plane
I don't know when I'll stop writing again
I won't be writing on a paper plain
I know I will continue to write my pain
Using techs like tablets and cellphones
Whenever I have time all alone at home.
I am giving out poems like I am insane
I don't know when I'll feel good in my brain
I am thankful to people who encouraged me to write
I don't know what I would have done in my life
Wanting to say something but no one to listen
I know my spirit now shines and glistens.
I am leaving on a poet's train
I don't know when I'll write the next refrain.

A RECORD

Good morning World
Good morning Zimbabwe
I know things are hard for all of us
But there's nothing like waking up to a new day
Another day another life
Forget your angst for a moment
Forget your snarky negative comment
And just think some as of yesterday died
Some as of yesterday at funerals cried
But you the chosen one
Have another day of fun
Go on run
Write that pun
You are chosen
My cousin
Wherever you are
No matter how far
Spread the love
Let it come
It's beautiful to be alive
To finally arrive
At this day
I say
At this hour
Life is ours
This minute
I mean it

This second
A record

ACROSTIC ACROBATT

At the moment of writing this verse
Clouds of dust rise in my universe
Rising to befuddle my oblaganta
Obliterating my mind's Magna Carta
Stopping me from writing prose
Trying to dull my smell of a rose
I will not be handicapped though,
Cannot be tricked an...aa.. anymore.
At least my brain is hard as a brickbat
Cleverly simulating a nebula acrobat
Rebooting my scholarly intuition
Operating my rhyming institution
Building my personal confidence.
And preparing my own defense
To this poetry journey to Venus
To enjoy "The Merchant of Venus"

VOYAGE OF ME'SCOVERY

The journey to find myself will never end.
The starting point unknown
At the end I am reborn

I wander in the galaxy of my mind
Billions of permutations and combinations
Decision algorithms are moving targets.

I search for my soul
Then, my spirit
And whence the two reside

So, here I am, an entity of mysteries
In self-knowledge hysteresis
When I think I have arrived, the journey begins delayed.

A voyage to my happenstance.
My consciousness
Voyage of me'scovery

A JOLLY GOOD FELLOW

From birth till death
He stands by me
Omnipresent wherever I go
Sometimes saying no
When I want to say yes
Under duress.

Five-foot six
Not tall, but dark and handsome
Been together through the war
And more
First time I met the fairer sex
He said make sure she will never be your ex

My lady is still my wife
And that's what he likes.
This guy you will never see
Never next to me
But, he's here in me
A jolly good fellow

I DON'T KNOW THE PEOPLE I KNOW

I thought it would be easy to know people
After all everywhere I look there are people
In my moments of happiness, there are people
In anguish, caused by people, there are people
Everywhere, there are people, people, people

I have met all kinds of people,
Friendly fiendish enemies
Strange estranged lovers
Unkind kindred relations
Quaint quality acquaintances

I "know" a lot of people
Turns out all of them are strangers
The people I know, I don't know if they know what I
know
Now I know
I don't know the people I know

IS THIS EVEN A POEM?

I started to write before I became a poet.
Actually, I did not know I was a poet
One day a poet called a spade a spade
Called me a poet and I became a poet
I think I am a poet, right?
Though not very bright.

I admire seasoned bards
Who doesn't find poetry hard
Putting the write words at the write time
Getting the write emotion
Making it seem like they took a portion
Like magic, the best words in the world unfurled.

I am sad though
I don't know
The more I read others the more I am bothered
Like I am losing my spontaneity
The ability to have thoughts flow raw from my brain to
pen to a poem.
I love what I read and am full of admiration
But I realize I can never be like anybody else except me
And that's how it's gonna be.

English is not my first language
But I do manage
I put my thoughts across

And sometimes make people cross
But, I miss that unbridled freedom
When I am master of my poetic kingdom.
I got to stop now
I don't know how
My feelings I pour 'em
But, I wonder, is this even a poem?

THAT DAY WAS MY DAY

I wrote a verse
This verse
Making me smile.
And loved my new lying style

My stomach growled
Troubled
Enzymes playing hunger games
My forehead in flames
Running a fever like a river flowing sweat
My short life under threat.

Spousal concern deep
No sleep
Taken to the doc
He cracked a joke.
Ran some tests
Said it was probably vaccine side effects.

I lay around pretending
Like my world was ending
Far from the madding crowd,
And my nagging spouse

That day was my day
I decided to say
There was an itch all over my body

Full of hypochondriac antibodies

I WROTE THIS POEM

Day four in the wilderness
Looking under every rock
Every cave trying to be brave
It's like everything had abandoned me
Everything except the air I breathed
The sun glared at my lack of ideas
The birds stopped singing
It was so dead quiet my ears were ringing
I looked up a mopane tree for inspiration
Its stoicism gave me perspiration
Its bare branches pointed up high in surrender
Then I remembered
I had not eaten since I ventured into the forest
and I had not had a rest
I was starting to hallucinate
Seeing mirages made of sonnets and ballads
My mind losing its balance
I sat down trying to focus
Guiding my mind on its locus
Why was I in the jungle?
Four days had been a bungle
After some meditation
Four deep gulps of ventilation
I remembered I went to find ideas
Ideas for a poem
A poem for a competition
I decided to do a petition

To my brain
To remain sane
And wrote this poem.

LIFE

Live it
It's short
For
Everyone

Love
Is
For
Ever

Live
In
Fairness
Everyday

Look
In and out
For
Earth

Life
Is
Finite,
Ends

ANOTHER DAY, ANOTHER LIFE

Happy celebrations
My cat Mambokatsi (Queen Cat) has kittens
She's been strutting around rotund
Proudly displaying her burgeoning bulge
Every time you walked past her dining place, she would
purr expectantly for food We are now experienced in
cat births
Having learnt the hard way
When her purr becomes hauntingly melancholic, then
it's almost time
She follows you everywhere trying to communicate.
I suspect it's, "The kittens are coming. Please prepare
my maternity ward" The last time we ignored our queen
cat was a disaster
My bed being the most comfortable she simply
delivered on my bed.
What a beautiful mess laundering the bed linen.
The other time she delivered in my dog kennel and we
only found little evidence of the tiny kitts. Now we
know
When she starts purring frantically,
Follows you everywhere,
Stops eating for some hours,
Know it's time to bring forth life
I put a cardboard box in my daughter's bedroom
Added some clothing padding to line it up

Lifted up Mambokatsi, stroked her, and gently placed
her in the box
The queen cat sniffed here and there
Looked at me approvingly
I closed the door and let nature do its thing
And it did
The next time I opened the door there were four little
kitties and a proud mommy cat the amazing thing is
there were no signs of gooey after birth. Cats are
amazingly clean. Another day, another life

TECHNOLOGICAL PERVERSION

The fly you see may be a spy
The one you don't see maybe sly.
Walls had ears for many years
Now they can video record your tears
Panning, tilting in any direction
Deep state watching for insurrection.
Your fridge involved in a cold war
Maybe sending what you don't know.
The TV, the light bulb and CCTV
Are they not send digits to CCTV?
To China Central, to Google, to where?
Are you really fully aware?

Is that rat not a brat?
Rat poison no longer having an effect
Worse still your cellphone
Is that not a smart drone?
Monitoring you through and through
You think you are smart being someone's fool
Even your roof sheets are awake
During the day making electricity for you to bake.
But, that's not the worst
The worst in this world
This technological perversion
Are you sure your children are the correct version?
Are they not designer babies?
Born from tech-infused ladies?

They don't obey parents
Their tech knowledge is so current.
Let it be said
Be very afraid!

WINTER MOODS...

Everything is shy in winter
The sun shy alters its path in the sky
The moon peeps shy, behind curtains of clouds
Animals shy, hide in their burrows
Pretty girls whose thighs kept our adrenaline going
All covered up
Shy
Even my wall thermometer is withdrawn
Playing hide and seek in its basement
Shy
Windows closed
Doors barricaded
Skin like chickenpox
Shying from exposure
My composure
A jersey inside
A jacket on the outside
Four layers of blankets
Wife melded to me
In the mood
In the hood
Winter moods.

HAVING FUN, HAVING PUN

He who hath no rhyme commits a crime
Fundies say rhyming kills the vibe
Disdain for matching sounds
Refrain is without grounds
Some make it a religion
Come to hate rhymes in all regions
At the start
Or end of the art
Poem rhymes
There are cries
Doesn't rhyme it's good
Easily understood
It's really easily just a reaction
To an action
Left lobe of the brain rebelling
Sound patterns repelling

Let's start a rebel movement
To cause improvement
In the attitude
And Latitude
To which rhyming is accepted
And not excepted
And recite our motto
For our mojo

Let us rhyme

Make us smile
The simplicity
Multiplicity
Duplicity
Audacity
Of rhyme
That time
Makes us young again
Something to gain
Like little kids
Satisfy the need
Pranking
Skanking
Having fun
Having pun

WORDS

His father used words
Words that added a decade to the boy's age
At eight he was eighteen on his father's rage range
Words out of this world
WORDS!

Words part of a paternal arsenal
Words a pestilence with a mouth of its own
Words from lips trilling in fatherly recusal
Words propelled by inebriated vocal cords
Words with hardness
Words with harshness

The boy's spirits never broke
He never spoke about WORDS
Wrote WORDS in prose
WORDS in poetry
Words out of this world
WORDS

THIS POEM

I am writing this poem on the fly
To enter this contest I will try
If I don't succeed I won't cry
I will still be a poet by the by

Why do we write
day and night
Always acting right
Picking a fight

Poetry is a calling
When things are falling
The world appalling
The canvas is a-calling

You say every day
You pray
For things to stay
Gay

That's poetry
Better than raising poultry
Poems
Pour 'em

WHEN YOU SAID YES! YES! YES!

Hippos yawned with disinterest

Not the slightest interest

Killers my foot!

Like they understood what was afoot

Crocs were basking on the riverbank

But I wasn't afraid, to be frank

I was afraid of what you'd say

What you'd say on that day.

When the question I popped

When I proposed

You and I in a canoe

"Can love me, can you?"

When you said yes! yes! yes!

I felt totally blessed

DO I?

Do I make you sad?
Do I make you bad?
Do I make you mad?
Act like your dad?

Do I make you cry?
Do I make you lie?
Do I make you sigh?
Make you high?

Do I make you weep?
Do I make you weak?
Do I make you speak?
Make you meek?

Do I make you laugh?
Do I give enough?
Do I make you rough?
Make you tough?

Do I make you lost?
Do I make you host?
Do I make you cost?
Make you toast?

Whatever you think
Whatever you feel

What I do I do for love
I do for love
Do for love
For love

DOCTOR DOCTOR THERE IS A POEM IN MY HEAD

Doctor doctor, there is a poem in my head
If I don't write it down my forehead will implode, I am afraid
I have had the problem for the last six months
When it afflicts me, I just want to write, can't do much
What is the diagnosis doctor I am going crazy?
Not much work at home, at the shop, or the farm, I am getting lazy

It's addictive?
With rum (rhyme)additives?
How does one get it Doc and is it curable?
It makes me speak like a freak in parables?
Makes me speak in metaphors?
Tell me Doc, why is it so?
Oh my God, there are many strains?
Some with gothic names so strange?

Thank God, I seem to have only a few mutations
Most in their gestation
There's freestyle poeting
The one making me laugh the limerick poeting
The one making me silly the clerihew poeting
The fixed temperature acrostic poeting
Maybe also a ballade poeting
And a sonnet poeting

So how do I get cured of this malady causing the ballade?
There is no cure, I just keep writing and eating more pudding (poetry)and salad. Thank you, Doc
Thanks for the talk

DON'T LET

Don't let
Anyone brings you down
And treat you like a clown

Don't let
Anyone stops you
And treat you like a fool

Don't let
Anyone makes you doubt your dream
And treat you like you are short of steam

Don't let
Anyone's opinion be your ultimate guide
And treat you like you have no pride

'Life is too short
Your retort!

'DON'T PLAY ME'

Mmmmm...He wondered
He pondered
He was not liked much in his life
Wherever he went he was disliked
Some said he was brusque
Domineering
A little impatient
When he spoke he shot from the hip
Quickdraw fire with ire

The result is he had few friends
All his life it had been a trend
The few he had, though, were good
They understood
He meant well
His mind rang a bell
When someone wasted his time
And took him on a fool's errand
He would say

'I don't call for folks to like me'
'Just to pay me'
'Not to play me'
'Don't play me'

DON'T STOP

At the end is a new beginning
On the way you find are other ways
Everything seems to change to remain the same anyway
Acceptance includes non-acceptance
Inductance the other form of reluctance
So long as you never look the beast in the eye,
for it will absorb your spirit and soul, yes, it will try

Stand in your position and absorb your surroundings till
you become one. Defeat is a state of mind the victor in
front is behind because he won
He is already down before it's said aloud
Develop a sixth, a seventh, and as many senses as your
life force allow

Spend time on your own in the forest standing still for
hours
Those who observe will understand you are not a
coward
Sitting by a stream bank watching the water cascading
down
will infuse music of the stream you won't frown.

The difficult and the easy incline each other.
A difficult situation is a small bother
If there is life there is hope
If there is a will there is scope

You will cope
Carry on

Don't stop

DOORS DOORS DOORS DOORS

Doors doors doors doors
I have been through many of those
Some doors led me to 'JAWS'
Loan sharks on great white floors.

Some doors lead nowhere
Some lead somewhere
Some doors you're not aware
The door is actually door ware

Some doors open one way
Like non-return valves from Norway
Others open some day
Some doors open every day.

Some doors are not for mortals
Will lead you to strange portals
Like a throttle
Some doors can lead you to a pothole.

Doors doors doors doors
Before you open those doors
Make sure you know
On the other side is a floor

WROTE PROSE

The sun rose

Then the moon rose

Bloomed the rose

Despite all those

I continued to doze

My life froze

Just because

I had no cause

To pause

I reposed

Close

To the hospital

To the ward

Due to Covid

Not to be bored

Wrote prose

EQUAL

Give me an equal fight
Equal right
Equal rice

Give me equal seed
Equal feed
Equal need

Give me equal oil
Equal soil
Equal toil

Give me equal race
Equal space
Equal pace

Give me an equal vote
Equal note
Equal home

Give me equal equal
Equal equal
Equal

ERROR MESSAGE IN MIRROR?

These days I look in the mirror
I see a new era
Something is wrong
My feeling strong
I don't see a reflection of myself
Is it a gnome or is it an elf?
This effigy
This refugee
An alien visitor
An avatar
Ecdysis?
Metamorphosis?
Whatever it is
I don't like this

Is it old age?
At the stage?
Hair grey
Temper frayed
Impatient
A patient
On life support pills
Depressing thrills
I fear lasses
Wear glasses
My eye
Am I?

Seeing me in the mirror?
Error message in the mirror?

68

EVERY

For years I blamed my mum
For leaving me when I was young
What I did not understand
There was a plan so grand

Now I have come of age
I have reached the crucial stage
What I thought important in life
Now I just take in my stride

Even if my children disowned me now
I would just wipe sweat off my brow
And carry on living till my last day
I'd be sad but have not much to say

If my wife of decades decided to leave
I would brood but continue to live
For I know I will never be alone
God provides me a permanent home

Every child is my child
Every bride my bride
Every mother my mother
Every man my brother

As long as you are living
To you love I will be giving

I will share the little I have
This is how we should behave

EVERY CHILD

The gynae mumbled something
Something which to me sounded like nothing
A cyst and what was this?
I thought it was his thesis

As far as I was concerned it was time for multiplication
and replication, we went home with our complications
Years went by without fruits
We had to face the truth.

We went to heaven and hell
From prayers then spells
Mental hospitals ports of call
Until it dawned nothing would help us cope.

It dawned that there were many children
It dawned they needed kindred
It dawned we could adopt
It dawned we could love them and adapt, and so

Every child I chide is mine in time
Every child I love is mine in life
Every child I care for is mine in time
Every child I give pride to is mine in life.

EVERY TIME

Every sixty seconds
I think of you sixty-six times
In my heart, I keep a record

Every sixty minutes
I speak your name sixty-six times
When I say I love you I mean it

Every twenty-four hours
I phone you twenty-two times
This beautiful love affair is ours

Every one week
I miss you eight days a week
"Eight days a week I love you" so to speak

And every month
The monthly cycle begins again
Just wanna say I love you very much

EVERYDAY LOVING FOR EVERYDAY PEOPLE.

Everyday loving for everyday people.
That's my promise to you if you be my woman
Together we will share the good and the bad
Work together to put our savings in a piggy bank

That's my promise to you if you be my woman.
We will fill our modest home with beautiful children
Work together to put our savings in a piggy bank
Every opportunity shakes the piggy upside down and
enjoy ourselves.

We will fill our modest home with beautiful children.
Together we will share the good and the bad
Every opportunity shakes the piggy upside down and
enjoy ourselves. Everyday loving for everyday people.

FAR FAR AWAY

I am standing at the shore
Realizing more and more
That I am at the interface
At the coal face
So, to speak
Anticipation at its peak

Behind me are fifty-six years of bruises
A litany of defunct truisms
None of them truthful
None of them fruitful
Turns out it was a game
A lame game for the tame

My father told me to obey rules
Rules are not for fools, he crooned
But now I feel real thrill here
Standing facing the unknown without fear.

Unlike Lot's wife
I've no urge to look back to my previous life
Doesn't matter what things the future brings
The cacophony of verbal abuses in my soul rings

I am going away
Far far away
To another country
A country of poetry.

YOU CANNOT WIN

When a mortal fights science
The mortal is silenced
You cannot win
No matter your whim
Science is the aggregation of life
Silence the aggravation of strife

When nature tells you to jump
Jump because there is a hump.
When nature says lie still
There is something out to kill
You
True

Don't argue
Argue
At your peril
Puerile
When science says wear a mask
Do the task

Your religious belief
Is no relief
When a mortal fights science
The mortal is silenced
You cannot win
No matter your whim

YOU AND YOU AND YOU AND YOU

Before I sleep I wanna thank some people
I am looking through a personal peephole
Some are alive
Some have arrived
To some place I never been
Where they are never seen

My wife is my life
Always there through my strife
My stepmom who stepped in to be my mom
My kids, daughter, and son
The villagers at the farm
To them, I stretch my forearm

My new family on Poem Hunter
We can have beautiful poetic banter
From all corners of the earth
Let's have fun merriment and mirth
Our poems harbinger of peace
I hope with a poem like this

You all feel my special thank you
For just being you and you and you
I thank you
You and you and you and you

WRITE IT DOWN

My communications professor asked.
'Between the words kikiriki and oumbooloomboo which
one sounds male and which sounds female? '
It was unanimous that the former was male
The latter was female.
It did not matter what language you speak. This was true
universally.

There is verbal communication and non-verbal
communication.

What makes poetry wonderful is that we write our
thoughts down. We want to communicate something.
Non-verbal communication is not the best way to
communicate with a bard.

Write it down.

Subliminal messaging is understood, though rude, it is
non-verbal communication. Completely unnecessary.

WRITE A POEM

Sleep
Dream
When you wake up
Write a poem

Bath
Go to work
At break time
Write a poem

Have lunch
Meet people
Chat
Write a poem

Knock off
Travel
Get home
Write a poem

Eat supper
Relax
Watch TV
Write a poem

Go to bed
Take a rest

And encore
It's all there in the poems

Love letters
Apologies
Epitaphs
Odes
It's all there in the poems

WONDERFUL WORLD

I trod down the road because I could not afford a Ford Ranger. The danger of a stranger being the arranger of a rambler is that he finds it a bender trying to explain that Jesus was born in a manger and starts to behave like an avenger instead of seeing things done out of fun by human beings as being sins leading to pins being stuck in their souls. That's all!

Crossing the crossing was a toad followed by a poisonous snake and out of fear of making a mistake of carrying the frog's cross I veered to the side in fear, wishing I had a ride I would have been proud to pride myself in. Poor frog panting like a dog dodged the reptile while I hid indeed afraid of being bitten by the viper, which was hyper and hyperventilating like an amphibian of Namibian origin, cornered in Nambia not far from Zambia not far from Zimbabwe. There was a simple way for the amphibian from toad to outsmart and outrun the ravenous raving rapacious reptile whose hunting maneuvers were outmoded. Just sitting on a toadstool seat still and praying and saying to the Maker of all things great and small, that frog will block its croaking poking, and mocking of all living things, including invisible beings like aliens, spirits, apparitions, ghosts, and gods. God! Toad needed saving from the hyper viper! Oh, God! The snake was all coiled up in a ball nothing could foil him from ending the afraid Freddy frog except a miracle and a miracle did happen.

I strode to the toad across the road and with a fake rubber snake strobe confused the serpent of doom. In the gloom, the snake stood still, no longer in the mood. It unwound itself like an unread book on the shelf, shook its head in disbelief, and took a hike just missed by a bike rode by a biker called Mike. I picked up the frightened toad and slid it in my pocket ostensibly for its protection, but I knew that a supper of frog legs would be new in my stew that evening.

What a wonderful, fair just, and equitable world!

WITH YOU

You can run and hide
But I will be with you
You can take a bus ride
Pretend you're part of the crew
My words you take offense
We no longer talk over the fence

You can loathe my lack of tact
Even bar my phone calls
Stop talking as a matter of fact
That's not going to work at all
The fact will still remain
I will always be in your brain

Where you are I am with you
In your mind and you in mine too

I will never you stalk
I just want to you talk
I will take a long walk.
From you and all the folk
But you will not find peace
The undeniable fact is this

Where you are I m with you
In your mind and you in mine too

WINTER MOODS

Everything is shy in winter
The sun, shy, alters its path
The moon, shy, peeps behind curtains of clouds
Animals, shy, hide in their burrows
Pretty girls whose thighs kept adrenaline going
All covered up
Shy?
My thermometer subdued
Shy
Mercury playing hide and seek in its lower basement

Windows closed
Doors barricaded
Skin like chickenpox
Shying from exposure

My new composure;
A jersey inside
A jacket outside
Four layers of blankets
Wife melded to me
In the mood
Winter moods.

WHEN YOU CHANGE YOUR MIND

When you change your mind
Hopefully, the hands of time will be still
In all certainty, you will be left behind

In all certainty, you will be left behind
The time you take is a fleeting moment
In the scheme of things, it flashes you blind

When you change your mind
Just remember I have a mind too
Common ground we may never find.

In all certainty, you will be left behind
Some things, if it feels right, do it
Intuition maybe your best guide

When you change your mind
The road you took may lead nowhere
'The road not taken' having been fine

Life is full of choices all the time
Some choices are for better for worse
When you change your mind
In all certainty, you will be left behind

WHEN I WAS YOUNG

When I was young my dad was very strict
He didn't want me to be a thug in the street
My father taught me the importance of timekeeping
The bad side of lying to get out of situations by fiddling

He didn't want me to be a thug in the street
When I was young my father was never thrifty
My father taught me the importance of timekeeping
The good side of keeping my word without quibbling

When I was young my father was never thrifty,
Or, the bad side of lying to get out of situations by
fiddling
But, the good side of keeping my word without
quibbling.
When I was young my dad was very strict

WHEN THE HEART CALLS

When the heart calls
A man always falls
A woman always walks tall
Like there is no issue at all

When the heart calls
Language is no issue at all
It is the same for all
In love or out you fall

When the heart calls
Irrationality also calls
Decisions don't make sense at all
Using emotion above all

When the heart calls
The heart calls
Just answer all calls
The heart calls

WHEN I WALK ALONE

88

When I walk alone in the valley of flowers
I see the splendor of nature and its powers
Flowers of all sizes, shapes, and colours
Nodding contentedly in the breeze for hours
The aroma and scent sublime
My serenity peaking in this Sub-Saharan clime

In the distance cows, heads bowed grazing gracefully
Next to them, goats guarding on the grass in rows like a
class
Sheep sheepishly sipping water at the pond fondly
bleating a beat
Male donkeys unashamedly lusting after their ass lasses
Only thing missing in this beautiful beast feast palaver is
my lover.

WHAT IF?

What if things were not what they are?
Would I have come this far?
What if I was not a poet?
How to write poems I didn't know?
Would I be taking a fifth anti-hypertension pill?
Would my feet be swelling still?

Whenever I write that little verse
I feel my life force moving in reverse
Away from certain morbid death
Giving me more time on this beautiful earth
Fellow humans come away with me
Come do poetry where medical assurance is free

WEAPON OF CHOICE

Poet observes the world moving
Over years sees nothing improving
Every suggestion made crushed
Tyrants having throats slashed
Workers abused at workplaces
Entire areas vanish without traces
All this annoys the poet no end
Poet wants to stop the trend
Only that he has no means to fight
No means to make things right
Out of a desire to do something
For the sake of unknown someone
Choice is made to write a verse
Highlighting the state observed
One, two, three gripping stanzas
In effect the power of a Panzer
Causing people to have a voice
Every poet weapon of choice

WHAT A SHAME

Is it a clever man who distorts occurrences of past events to assume higher degrees of a pedigree with sumptuous artificial sophistry?

This gives credence to an adage propounded by one prominent African president, himself, the epitome of the intrinsic contradictions of hackneyed storytelling amplified by he who benefits from his own lies. The Son of Africa opined that it is not critically important to fret about where you have been, but where you are and where you are going.

True true. After all the history you are taught is untrue.

The history taught is the worst form of mental slavery. It's a mystery why billions take propaganda for a fact. They recite, with excitement, the script, to the exclusion of any intellectual critique.

And, yet the truth is hidden in plain sight.

What a shame.

WALKING IN A BLIND WORLD

Walking in a blind world
People with eyes who can't see
Their range limited by assumptions
Multimedia slavery
Flashing words and pictures
Doctored reality
A comfort zone
Fiction
Friction

Is it true then reality can be made?
Like the reality of the sun
That it rises in the east
We could have called it west
The sun will still rise
Manufactured Consent
A convenient way to live
Easy to accept
The truth to except

Stubborn like the sun
The truth
Send a Parker Probe
Get up real close
It's expensive
It's not easy
The luminosity opens our eyes for posterity

Regrettably, we believe someone's a weird word
Walking in a blind world

WALK AWAY

"If you love something
You must let it go
If it comes back, it's yours
If it doesn't come back
t'was never yours"

I'm letting you go
Cause I love you so much
You are perfection
A flawless diamond
Beyond my horizon
In my horror zone

Fly away my love
Go your way for good
My love is infinite
My emotions finite

Can't stand watching you
walk away for real
the simple harmonic motion
of your beautiful backside
walking away
with another man

So, walk away
Walk away.

WAKING UP TO THE UNKNOWN

Times have changed
I used to wake up to a pre-planned day
Now I wake up to the unknown.
Nothing surprises me anymore

It could be;
'The neighbour died last night'
The guy I last saw the midnight
Full of life
Going on about what he disliked.

It could be; 'There is no more work'
There is a shutdown due to a virus
Or the government has changed
Overnight
I just shrug my shoulders and think 'Oh well,' that's
alright.

There's something constant though,
The love of God is something I know.
Come rain come shine
I know with God I'll be fine

VOICES OF CHOICES

I have an invisible "friend" on my left shoulder
Helps me to make a decision
At the fork in the road, I ask my "friend"
To help me make up my mind with precision.
Alas, oft times my adviser behaves like a fiend
A rival sits on the other shoulder acting bolder
Then I am embroiled in a dilemma contest
Suffering the proverbial should I or should I not own
test.

I hear voices giving choices
Voices of choices
To be or not to be
To see or not to see
To do or not to do
For you or not for you
Thank God I make the final choices
Thank God they are just voices

UNSHAKABLE

At daybreak I expected the sun to rise
I was in for a surprise
There was an eclipse of the sun
Like on this day the end was nigh
The sun flipped over its rays shining into the cosmos
bright
On a clear cloudless day, it was quite a sight

The moon that night, its light so hot
The stars in constellation consternation they brought
The ground I stood on transparent
Making volcanic eruptions at the earth's core apparent
The stationary wind smelling of incense
Everything not making sense

I stood in wonderment
Like an explorer in a wonderland
Making the first contact
My soul intact
All my vital signs standard
Never feeling stranded
Unshakable

UN...

Sometimes I feel UNwanted.
Even UNloved
I wonder why I am treated UNfairly
Like I am UNappreciated

Many people are Unfriendly
Some Unwelcoming
Their hostility is UNwarranted
Because I am quite UNassuming

I am happy go luck UN restrained
Open-minded UNbiased
My loving is UNlimited
Though it is Unrequited

But I am UNfazed.
I shall go the UN
To find out why I am UNpopular
Perhaps I will be UNchained

I can begin life anew
Reforming for you
Something new
Changing UN to NU

UNKNOWN

Technology is changing our world in a bad way. Which is good. Like MJ sang "I'm bad! ", meaning he's good. At the click of a rodent-named device, a potato couch can just crouch around a collection of nano transistors, smart light-emitting diodes, and have the world at its feet.

Technology has made our lives more equal due to its pervasive nature. People are more appreciative of other people's real-life struggles and with Google getting real-time detailed street images, what then is the point of being a tourist when you have been there without going there.

People are staying indoors while they go out and in part COVID has made things worse by making governments enforce a dystopian lockdown rule. Although we are highly connected, we have become highly detached. This is retrogressive and soon the negative effects of going there without physically going there will take its toll.

Human beings are a prejudicial self-hating species who wish their humanoid clone ill will and hiding behind diodes, nano transistors, and using a lifeless rodent will make it easier to hate each other. After all, you don't have to look into my eyes when I die You don't witness my lifeblood oozing out when I die.

You just click my life away!
A rodent master getting his pay!

Halfway round the globe
Hundreds of miles in the sky
There is a cyborg watching with a strobe
Relaying macabre messages high
cyborgs intricately wired together
Sending death knell images, it gathers
the messages decoded in real-time
to a youthful man about to do a real crime

In the sky halfway round the world
A hi-tech aluminum bird is unfurled
answers to a joystick of a psychopath
the whims of an imperial sociopath
Under its belly is deadly ordnance
Something grotesquely deadly but ordinary
The bird's eye view is searching for a kill
The young man nonchalantly feeling a thrill

A hapless man has been labeled a terrorist
He is enjoying his freedom as a tourist
a chip placed in his phone
guiding the aluminum falcon home
high up above the sky on a lovely day
he talks to God differently as he prays
An instant flash sucks in all his air
burns all around him singe his hair

100

TWO WRONGS MAY MAKE A RIGHT

Two wrongs may make a right
If someone comes blustering
Give them measure for measure a fight.

Give them measure for measure a fight
They want pacificity at an advantage
Give a taste of their medicine to teach them what's
right

Two wrongs may make a right
What were they thinking when they wronged you?
When they deliberately put you in your plight?

Give them measure for measure a fight
Respect comes from getting and giving.
The balance of action and reaction gives better insight.

Two wrongs may make a right
Disequilibrium begets equilibrium
Those who start a fight must be shown the light.

For a future equitable and bright
Give to Caesar what belongs to him and this could be
payback
Two wrongs may make a right
Give them measure for measure a good fight.

INSOMNIA

Its three a.m.
Awake I am
Lying down no aim
There's light rain
And a power cut
Ceiling fan is out
It's become hot
Sleep I can not
My mind goes to poetry land
I stretch out my hand
Looking for my phone
With muted ringtone

World time is three a.m.
Restless I am
It's very hot
I am slowly stewing in a pot
I go to the kitchen
I wonder where's my kitty and kitten
I change over inverter
To bring solar power on its better
I check the slow cooker
It's been doing samp the wife it took her
lots of pleading to get me to check it
I am not keen like I don't eat it

Fan running

Mind running
No more sleeping
No more dreaming
I travel far in my mind
To find a poem to write
That's what I do
Write something new
When I can't sleep
So, my sanity I keep
So, I wrote these verses of twelve lines
Then went back to sleep finally.

TRUTH

Freedom of expression is conditional upon consummating your ideas with those of the standards. Whose standards? The way it's been done always. What the whole world has accepted as a fact. A fact-based on empiricism or based on imperialism?
Let's take the fact to the lab and have it certified free of emotion or conjecture or belief or faith. No. These things cannot be done in the laboratory. You must just justly verily have faith. Ummm, what if there is irrefutable empirical evidence that it is because of this lack of query and inquiry that has led to fanatical genocides and conflicts among the same people based on doctored documents politicized to suit a particular narrative as we have seen MSM do? We must still accept because everyone accepts. No!

The reason why nature gave me medulla oblongata is so I reason, I think, to save myself and my environment and all those things in earth's firmament. It would be a dereliction of my natural duty to accept every truism in life without interrogation because that's how things are. Truth is not afraid of interrogation and criticism because it does not change. After all the trials, tribulations, and rigorous exhaustive assessment, a truth remains because it IS. It doesn't matter if one person or two billion people believe in the truth. It will be what it IS.
I rest my case.

Exeunt.

A TRIP TO SPACE

Trudging on a road so long
With multi-dimensions all wrong
It would twist your feet and neck
On the way are many a wreck
You have one chance to choose a way
Where you are at, you cannot stay.

You choose a way without a way
Seemingly leading astray
Unlike other routes, it's harder its longer
Despite its steep ascent descent, it has a ladder much
stronger
And only three dimensions
And a litter of three-headed dalmatians.

You make good progress going nowhere
It seems futile you are worse for wear
But you realize there is one faithful canine
Sometimes getting big sometimes small and a Grand
Canyon
Concave, convex, and flat mirrors making a tunnel to
destination X
Your dying will wish you had an axe

An axe to grind
An axe to break all mirrors to the ground
An axe to chop your dog meat

An axe to test your heartbeat
An X and Y cartesian coordinate
An X factor type android mate

Tired; so, you lay down to sleep
Your sleep really deep
You dream you are in a room
A room designed like a tomb
Your subconscious replays every detail
For your trip to space, you had to be detained.

TRIP TO INDIA

Around the world in one week
Meeting people hearing them speak
It's good to take some time off
I flew to India from work being off
The land of curry and rice
Spices so hot and so nice

In the morning a hearty breakfast
After "Namaste" we dug in fast
Delicious food great company
Like I was royalty on the SS Campari
Had delicious Indian sweet cakes
"Dhanyawad! " I said for courtesy sakes

I savoured Rusgullah sweet cakes
Also Gulab jam and Sandesh tastes
The best was Mathura delight
So deliciously heavy but so light
I tried to phone Dillip K Swain
But he was busy on PH with RM Smith

TIP OR TRIP

I took a trip where I had to tiptoe
The tip of my nose tipping quietly
Tip of my eyes peeled tripping for danger
At the tipping point of midnight
I walked tipsily to the tip of the stairs
Knocked softly at a door with the tip of my knuckle
tipped.
Stealth was the operative word I had been tipped.

My surprise tripped because she had got a tip
She tiptoed to the door
Opened it and tipped a flower pot
I tripped and almost tipped over the tip of the
balustrade
She caught me with the tip of her finger
To my surprise, she kissed me with the tip of her lips
And said her mum and dad had gone on a trip.

TOO SOMETHING

My skin used to be thin
It has acquired layers of indifference to be this thing
Whatever thing I did
It was like I was stupid

It was too this or too that
The drink was too flat
The tea too weak or too hot
Even if anything was, it was not

I use my thickened skin for defense
Going about never taking offense
They try to put me down
All I hear is, smiling like a clown,

This is too something
That is too something
Too something
Too something

TOGETHER TILL DEAD

When you are gone
My heart leaves my chest
And stray so forlorn
I cannot find rest

Do not leave me alone
My mind leaves my head
I go berserk on the phone
Thinking you are in bed

When you are not with me
I feel bodily dismembered
My ribs feel dislodged free
I ask you do you remember

The love we shared
The price we paid
The oath we said
Together till dead

TODAY

Today is a special day
It's been long coming
I have been meaning to face up to this unique day
One of a kind days
Another time I will never find
On this particular day
The setting is just right
There is a cool soothing breeze
The sun not too hot,
not too cold like it's primed for this particular day
This day of days
The day seemingly chosen
Everything else frozen
Today I have the courage,
not Dutch but real.
The day to say what I feel
I know it's taken long
The urge to talk is strong
But I had to wait for this day
This momentous day to say,
that one in a million event,
is here no one can prevent.
This one day in a lifetime
This time is really mine
I dressed really well
In my tuxedo looking swell
Today I look into your eyes,

so, you know there are no lies
My right knee will kiss the ground,
will not check who is around.
My left knee will kiss the floor
I will bow a little more
On this fateful day
Hold both your hands
It's really been a long road
To remove this my load
I've had sleepless nights
Wondering if this day is right
Many what-ifs
Fear of unknown tiffs
Today I'm ready
My nerves are steady
Today I'm saying
"Marry me! "
Today.

CYBER POETIC TOBOGGAN

Let's take flight into outer space
Join the inevitable space race
With our poetic note pads
All poets old, new, lasses or lads

Let our poems go through that satellite
One corner of the world set alight
With rhymes, metaphors, and adverbs
The other corner of the world sending adverts

Let's send our poems to other galaxies
On every spaceship poem on balances
Ballads, sonnets, and free verse in digital form
our sadness and laughter reaching other life forms

Let's do a cyber poetic toboggan
In space a cyber poetic toboggan

Cyber poetic toboggan

Correct me if I am right or wrong
You should agree the evidence is strong
Beyond our solar system are people
Even we can't see them in a peephole
Refocusing our telescopes and probes
Promises to increase the probe-ability
Of us contacting other alien species

Everyone mentions this in speeches
Tourism in space now a possibility
In the future no longer just probability
Can we poets be left out of the race?
To make that life form sob and laugh
Out there teach them our way is tough
But we empathize we ruminate we cry
Oh, we are not perfect on earth we try
Going out of our way for each other
Going out of our way for father mother
And all the inhabitants of this world
Now to space our poems digitally unfurled

I COULD HAVE DIED

To think I could have died
How many would have cried
There are so many pretenders
Fawning love only to spite
Acting as if they are defenders
They say you're right
Then whisper you're stupid
Strike you with an arrow, not from Cupid

To think I could have died
How many would have tried
Tried to save me from the shame
Not given me the same
Bleeding my heart with deceit
My money there is no receipt
My time there's no refund
Just more and more demands

To think I could have died
I wonder who would've cried
She was there to apply heat
She was there to treat my wrist
Made sure I didn't take the wrong pill
Convulse sweat and be killed
Then she was awake with me
To make sure I was healed

TITANIC LOVERS

We used to be so so close
We used to be so so in love
Now you drifted drifted away
Like the Titanic far far from the bay

You have become so so cold
You used to be so so bold
Now you don't you won't face me
Like the Titanic, you are sinking out to sea.

Forgive me, love love, forgive me
Let us retrace embrace a love so free
Our love let's revive let's not let it nose dive
Like the famed famous Titanic, lovers let's survive
The turn, the season, the reason

Do you ever wonder when you will die? I do and I think
you do too.
Thank God we are made mortal,
to leave this earth go to another portal. I don't know
why people sob and feign sorrow
as if a beloved will rise again tomorrow.
When someone passes on,
It's time to go on the phone,
call for people to come to drink, eat and be merry,
because life is not a game of cat and mouse-like Tom
and Jerry.

No matter who you are, black, white
or whatever hue and colour,
we all end up silent at the parlour.

Who is he who says he be the master of another
human?
Who is she who says she be the queen among all
woman?
With all riches, the time reaches when you join the food
chain
like flotsam discharged to the flood plain.

I beseech you my brothers and sisters, significant others
and all creatures,
do good unto others and your soul will rest in peace,
your tombstone we will kiss.
We will have wine, whiskey, and beer and your passing
will be our cheer,
because the laws of death are not ours,
and bury you in hours. Such is life.

TIME MOVES ON

I used to do one-eighty degree splits
One finger push-ups
A practioner of Jeet Kune Do
One of the best
Even defeated a Brown belt
Had my own students
Now it's just a daydream
Time moves on in days

I used to be a young engineer
Designing electrical systems
To schools, churches, clubs
Even highrise buildings with lifts
Always willing to challenge the best
Now I am connected to the earth
driving to my farm every weekend
Time moves on in weeks

I used to worry about the future
About my retirement
Wanted to give my kids the best
Now it's just me and my spouse
In our house with our cat and dogs
Poetry is my new passion till death
Hurtling at 365 days per year
Time moves on in years

TIME IS NOT A JEALOUS COMMODITY

Time is not a jealous commodity
It moves surreptitiously for all
Tik tok tik tok tik tok goes the clock
Stealing the days of your life

It moves surreptitiously for all
Ready or not your time is gone forever
Stealing the days of your life
The best is to steal your moments in time

Ready or not your time is gone forever
Tik tok tik tok tik tok goes the clock
The best is to steal your moments in time
Because time is not a jealous commodity

WRITERS BLOCK

1.

Deluke wants to write a poem today
Alas, he has very little to say
Every rhyme he musters
Disappears faster
Deluke has given up, going out to pray

2.

Just in time

They say don't worry this is writer's block
I say no I need a poem by the clock
Got nothing to write
Because I am bright
I wrote some limerick on a cloth

Time

There is a concept severally understood called time.

Every race has its own concept of this elusive time

The Japanese believe and do things just in time,

even commit hara-kiri for failing to control time.

121

The West control, it believes might is right all the time.

The Chinese will do stuff slowly bide their time,

over thousands of years, they watch the unfolding time.

The most interesting slave masters of time,

are the Africans and their disregard of time.

Africans will get round to doing something sometime.

What use is it to control something as misunderstood as time?

Africa has everything it needs all the time.

Land, minerals, and everything people need especially time.

Time will tell whether African Wisdom will stand the test time.

THRILL AFTER THRILL

It starts with a word
That unique word in the world
It could be a noun, adjective, or verb
A collection of words turning to a verse then a reverb
Giving a thrill
Thrill after thrill

A stanza gives a picture
A glimpse, a tincture
You add detail
Shape and form like in retail
Images having a thrill
Thrill after thrill

A poem is born
Another verse clothes the bone
A life of its own
Like a rocket flown
Filling with thrill
Thrill after thrill

THIS THING CALLED KISSING

This thing called kissing
So easy you can do it with your eyes closed
The build-up to a first kiss is a unique experience
You can also do it with eyes open.

So easy you can do it with your eyes closed
It causes your heartbeat to increase in anticipation
You can also do it with eyes open.
If you are a first-timer closing your eyes is instinctive.

It causes your heartbeat to increase in anticipation
The build-up to a first kiss is a unique experience.
If you are a first-timer closing your eyes is instinctive.
This thing called kissing

THINK

You wear a straightjacket
Thoughts packed in a packet
Ideas locked in a mental prison
Desires defracted in a prism

It's a doctrine of absoluteness
Doesn't matter the truthfulness
You follow the dogma
And sit down on a dog mat

When you try to unravel the truth
They treat you like a common crook
"I was just thinking aloud! "
As if thinking is allowed.

Think about it
Think
About
It.

About
It
Think
It's about time you think.

THE.......

The fleas are biting
The dog is fighting
The sun is lighting
The man is shouting

The heat in kitchen
The skin is itching
The food is chicken
The dog is sniffing

The wife is cooking
The dog is looking
The man is crooking
The fowl is spooking

The poetry is stale
The poultry is pale
The canine on sale
The man drinks ale

THE TREE

So I was talking to my mopane tree
Its dark green nutritious leaves waving in the wind
Ready to feed the mopane worm for me
A delicacy I enjoy every time of the rainy season

The tree cautioned me though
Whispering in three language
That some species of worms are foreign I should know
Armyworm and stalk borer will cause damage

I smiled and whispered back in the same tongue
To the tree, my tree, my mopane tree
That my knapsacks are ready the pesticides primed in tonnes
Bring it on, creepy crawlers, let the battle begin

My mopane tree whispered in sadness and suspense
Said these chemicals are killing other beneficial creatures
My faithful bitch Booboo died last week of poisoning we suspect
The wise mopane tree tries to warn me and teach us

I listen to the whispering tree
Giving environmental advice for free
It speaks ecosystem language to me
It's behaviour guided by nature for all to see.

127

THE SUN

Today I spoke to the life-giving sun
The sun, smiling with moon face, spoke to me
The sun told me this time it will be a good run
The sun ordered El Nino to set me free
El Nina is coming to allay my fears
The sky will welcome her with rivers of tears

The sun asked if I had spoken to the soil
And made sure my mechanical friends were oiled
there was not much the sun could do
To ensure the earth was on my side too
I assured the sun that the earth was mine
The fertility, virility, and permeability was fine

I told the sun to tell the moon to respect the clouds
To hide behind the curtain of moisture but still be proud
coming out briefly to assure the owl there's life after
the storm
not to cause a high tide to upset El Nina's coming home
Yeah, today I spoke to the sun
I m going to the farm with El Nina arm in arm to have
fun

THE SOLITARY JOURNEY WE TRAVEL

The solitary journey we travel
Is a journey of unknown miles
Your date of arrival will unravel

Your date of arrival will unravel
On the day that you pass on
You will be covered in gravel.

The solitary journey we travel
You meet lovers you think you love
And strangers you can't love but marvel

Your date of arrival will unravel
The choices you make affect your journey
Bad choices may affect your arrival

The solitary journey we travel
Is full of excitement and risks
The usual risk and return trade-off

Peace be with you traveller
Don't be afraid to fall and rise
On the solitary journey, we travel
Because your date of arrival will unravel

THE RIVER CRIES

Many drowned therein, crying
Many insects caught up in the current, dying, crying
The birds came for a drink, snapped by the croc, crying
The little impala came to quench its thirst, died, crying
Predator after predator, savouring the cries, of victims
caught at the water's edge.
In the depths, the big fish makes the small cry, gurgle,
and die
Fishes cry, their spawn sumptuous meals
Plastic pollution, raw sewage, and other debris, making
the fishermen cry
Catching dead fish.
Don't be fooled by the placid stroll of the river
The life giver cries
The river cries.

THE REACH MAN

Familiarity with riches tempts
With the ability, you attempt
Everything has a price
Everyone bought with rice
Your loot playing the lute
The Pied Piper you dilute
Your perspective de facto reality
Corrupted system confers legality
You are the rich man
The reach man

The reach man
The rich man
Is it then that you know all there is to know?
Indigenous knowledge not at all?
Your point of view
Makes everyone your fool
Dissenters refrain
Suppressed without restraint

Rich man
Reach man
Preach man
Teach man
From your power
From your tower
The rich man

131

Alas, is the reach man

THE QUARANTINES

Thousands of years from now
People will kneel, pray and bow
Reading the newer New Testament
A new bible in the new firmament
A bible with stories from text old
Stories of Jesus also being bold

There will be stories of Egyptians
Stories of Israelis and Ethiopians
Stories of the Persia and Philistines
Even as far as Samoa and Philippines
The newer book about our quarantine,
having a section on "The Quarantines"

In it will be stories of faces distorted
Population countenances contorted
Baptized in seventy percent ethanol
Wounds in glycerine and ichthammol
Married couples in counter embrace
Clergy dazed cloaked in total disgrace

We are The Quarantines
Suffer silently the quarantine
Stories of "The Quarantines"
Told in the "The Quarantines"

133

THE ONE AND ONLY

There comes a time a boy becomes a man and this is my
time
I have been searching high and low, near and far
And now I am making you the one and only

And now I am making you the one and only
No more games, no more standing you up
Be rest assured you will never be alone

There comes a time a boy becomes a man and this is my
time.
I will be your friend and pillar of strength.
I will always be there to make you feel mine

And now I am making you the one and only
The one I will spend the rest of my life with
The one I will cherish and, like a delicate flower, hold
softly

There comes a time a boy becomes a man and this is my
time
No more youthful exuberance
No more involvement in petty crime

Be my love, I am asking you fondly
And I am asking you formally

There comes a time a boy becomes a man and this is my
time
And now I am making you the one and only

THIS MOOD

I am falling deeper into the sweetness of your love
I pretend to crawl out, but I am stuck in its cove
I am at that pure point of epiphany,
what I thought was epically funny,
is a reality in my life, a dream come true
Definitely, in this slide, I will pull through

It's true,
It's never too late to fall in love

I knew,
It was possible you would soon come

I see,
It's true you have finally arrived

It's me,
to make sure our love survives

Where do we meet on the dark street?
Where do we greet our love so sweet?
What is the passcode to your door?
How much love do I bring to your floor?
Are you coming with me for good?
Are we together in this erotic mood?

THE MISSION

It's deep
Pulse astronomic
Can't sleep
With such energy

Such enthalpy
The entropy
Atomic
Like Chernobyl

I m enthralled
Fusion of souls
At sub-atomic level
With molecular resonance

The mission
To give love
In every form
Though platonic

The precedent
The incident
Careless desire
Causing fire.

Tryst permissible?
Reversible?

May be so
But I remember Bhopal.

ABOUT THE AUTHOR

DELUKE MUWANIGWA

I was born on June 18, 1964 in southern Zimbabwe, in a village called Chivi, in Masvingo Province. At the time, Zimbabwe was under Ian Smith's government and a guerrilla war was in its infancy to free the country from colonial rule. I have scant memories of my early days, but the difficult rural life and occasional abuses I went through, stir sad memories in me sometimes. Some of it is captured in my poems.

In 1973 I moved to Zambia to escape the escalating bush war. In December 1977 my father inexplicably decided to immigrate back to the then Rhodesia at the height of the war and his nationalist activism eventually took his life in August 1979.

On April 18, 1980, Zimbabwe got its Independence from Britain. At that point, I went back to school to repeat my grade seven, passed, and went to Lord Malvern High School, in Waterfalls, a suburb of Harare, where I met my wife. Our affair started when we were in form two in 1982, she being 15 years old and I, being 18 years old.

We were in the same class for the 6 years of our secondary school, passed well, and went to the University of Zimbabwe. I studied electrical engineering and she studied pharmacy.

We are still together today, nearly 40 years later. We have two children, Dananayi and Mudiwa Nathasia.

The question on many peoples' minds may be; what's an electrical engineer doing writing poetry?. Beats me, but, it's something I have a natural passion for. I did not go to poetry school, though I wish I had, and I have learned poetry the hard way; through reading poetry and interacting with other poets on poetry fora. Enough said. Enjoy the poems.